Reading Roundabout

How to make a Mask

Paul Humphrey

Photography by Chris Fairclough

W
FRANKLIN WATTS
LONDON • SYDNEY

First published in 2006 by
Franklin Watts
338 Euston Road
London NW1 3BH

Franklin Watts Australia
Hachette Children's Books
Level 17/207 Kent Street
Sydney NSW 2000

© 2006 Franklin Watts

ISBN: 0 7496 6609 9 (hbk)
ISBN: 0 7496 6860 1 (pbk)

Dewey classification number: 731'.75

A CIP catalogue record for this book is available
from the British Library.

Planning and production by Discovery Books Limited
Editor: Rachel Tisdale
Designer: Ian Winton
Photography: Chris Fairclough
Series advisors: Diana Bentley MA and Dee Reid MA,
Fellows of Oxford Brookes University

The author, packager and publisher would like to thank the following
people for their participation in this book: Auriel and Ottilie Austin-Baker.

Printed in China

Contents

What you need

Do you like clowns?
Here's how to make a
clown mask.

These are
the things
you will need:

A large
paper plate

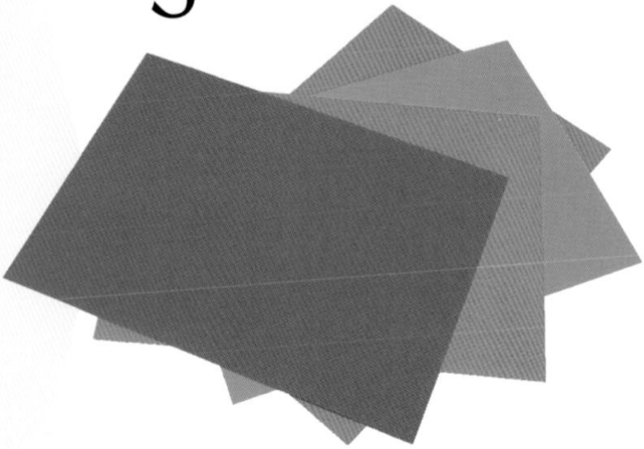

An eraser

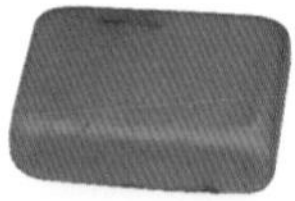

A pencil

Coloured card

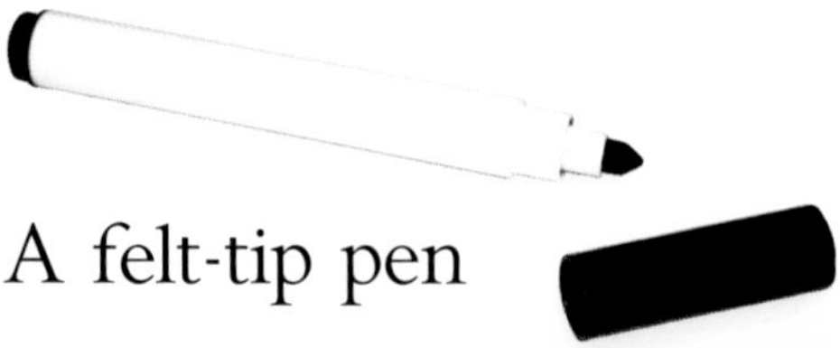

A felt-tip pen

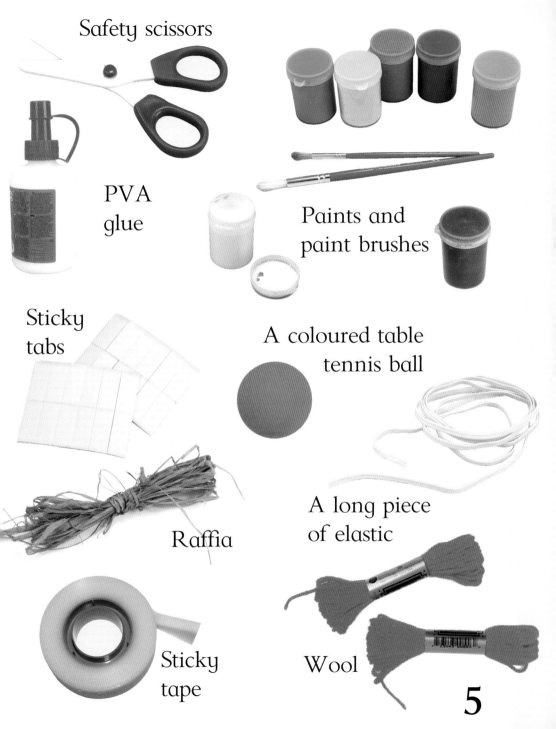

Safety scissors

PVA glue

Paints and paint brushes

Sticky tabs

A coloured table tennis ball

Raffia

A long piece of elastic

Sticky tape

Wool

5

Marking the eyes

First, paint the paper plate white.

Hold the plate against your face. Feel where your eyes are.

Ask a friend to mark where your eyes are with a felt-tip pen.

Cutting the eyes

Draw circles on the paper plate where your eyes are.

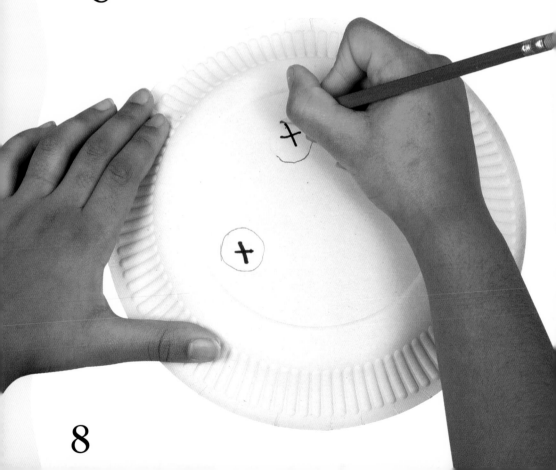

Then cut out the circles.

Making the mouth

Now ask a friend to draw where your mouth is.

Fold the plate in
half and cut out
the mouth
across the
fold.

Painting the eyes and mouth

Next, paint around the eye holes in bright colours.

Paint smiley lips
around the mouth.

Making the hat and bow tie

Cut out a
hat and bow
tie from
the card.

Decorate them with strips of card. Fix raffia to the hat with tape.

Making the hair

Cut the wool into strands.

Glue the wool to each side of the mask to make hair.

Fixing the hat and bow tie

Use sticky tabs to fix the hat and bow tie on to the mask.

Making the nose

To make the nose press on the table tennis ball until one edge is flat.

20

Then use sticky tabs
to fix the ball on to
the mask.

Wearing your mask

Use the pencil and eraser to make a hole on each side of the mask.

Thread the elastic through each hole.

Finally, tie
a knot in
each end.

Now
you can
wear your
mask!

Steps

Can you remember all of the steps to make your mask?

1. Mark and cut eyes.

2. Mark and cut mouth.

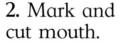

3. Paint eyes and mouth.

4. Make hat and bow tie.

5. Make and glue hair.

6. Fix hat and bow tie.

7. Make and fix nose.

8. Tie elastic.

9. Wear your finished mask.